An Attorney's Guide to the Collection of Bad Debts

3rd Edition

T0149503

An Attorney's Guide to the Collection of Bad Debts

3rd Edition

Robert L. Lewis, Esq.
and
Abraham J. Perlstein, Esq.

iUniverse LLC
Bloomington

AN ATTORNEY'S GUIDE TO THE COLLECTION OF BAD DEBTS: 3RD EDITION

iUniverse books may be ordered through booksellers or by contacting:

iUniverse LLC
1663 Liberty Drive
Bloomington, IN 47403
www.iuniverse.com
1-800-Authors (1-800-288-4677)

Because of the dynamic nature of the Internet, any web addresses or links contained in this book may have changed since publication and may no longer be valid. The views expressed in this work are solely those of the author and do not necessarily reflect the views of the publisher, and the publisher hereby disclaims any responsibility for them.

Any people depicted in stock imagery provided by Thinkstock are models, and such images are being used for illustrative purposes only.
Certain stock imagery © Thinkstock.

ISBN: 978-1-4917-0358-8 (sc)
ISBN: 978-1-4917-0359-5 (e)

Library of Congress Control Number: 2013914580

Printed in the United States of America

iUniverse rev. date: 08/29/2013

Contents

INTRODUCTION

When written in Chinese, the word 'crisis' is composed of two characters. One represents danger and the other represents opportunity.

—John F. Kennedy

How to Use this Book

An Attorney's Guide to the Collection of Bad Debts is meant to give readers a broad overview of debt-collection techniques, as well as to inform them of some popular debt-collection techniques used by attorneys. The reader should consider this book a type of debt-collection techniques catalog.

We authored this third edition so that it can be read easily and quickly during a day's commute to and from work. This third edition also contains revised copies of sample legal forms used to facilitate the collection of bad debts.

After reading this book, you will become aware of certain collection techniques, so that you can make an informed discussion with an attorney about potential options available to you.

This book is not to be considered legal advice, and is meant for general information purposes only. This book is not a substitute for the advice of legal counsel.

Chapter 1

TYPES OF
BAD DEBT CASES

I'll gladly pay you Tuesday for a hamburger today.

—Wimpy in *Popeye*

Litigation arising out of the collection of bad debts primarily involves actual disputes, but many cases center on the fact that one of the parties is having a money problem. Thus, winning a lawsuit is meaningless if you cannot collect any of the money which is due and owing.

Usually, when a customer and supplier/lender/borrower/ provider have a dispute about quality, amount or price, they will both seek to resolve the dispute in order to continue the relationship.

If the dispute cannot be resolved, then it involves either a serious difference of opinion or financial difficulties on the part of one of the parties. In our experience, most of the litigated commercial matters involve credit sensitivity.

Many cases that seem like mundane commercial matters revolve around the fact that one of the parties is lacking funds. Most of these cases develop when one of the parties-either the buyer or the seller-is running out of funds. In desperation, they will try to squeeze funds from their own customers, despite the cost of losing or alienating their existing customers. Similarly, it is like a drowning man who will grab on to anyone, and even pull them into the water, in a last effort to try to save himself. Set forth below are a few of the most common examples indicating that one of the parties is running out of funds,

A. A Consignment Becomes A Sale

You have an understanding with a supplier that you can always return goods you do not use. Since this had been a long-standing and successful arrangement, you do not hesitate to order goods you know you can return. Your supplier knows that there is a higher probability that you will use goods if they are readily available to you.

Suddenly, your supplier refuses to accept the return of the goods and insists that you pay for them. He informs you that the "return" policy is no longer in effect, and that it was your responsibility to be aware of the change. You tell him that you would never have ordered so many goods in that case. His response is that the situation is your problem, and that he needs the money. You next receive a Summons and Complaint from his attorney.

A similar scenario involves the retail store that carries jewelry or pictures on consignment from wholesaler. Basically, the wholesaler is using your store as his display window, and you rely on the wholesaler as your bank to finance your inventory. It is a mutually beneficial relationship until the wholesaler demands payment for the goods you" bought," and starts suit to collect.

Another related example involves the receipt of goods you never ordered. You are in the habit of ordering certain goods from a supplier. You now find that you are receiving more than you ordered, and that you are even receiving shipments of goods you never ordered. In such cases, you must come to understand that your supplier or wholesaler is attempting to increase sales by forcing you to take his goods, even if you never agreed to do so. This is the sign of a desperate person looking to obtain money from any source available. He may argue with you on commercial grounds, but you must be aware that he is simply desperate for money.

B. Inferior Goods

Your usual supplier starts substituting inferior goods for the quality of goods that you usually receive. Most of the time, this is done gradually, but it is plausible for this to happen suddenly. The supplier is cutting corners and saving money by sending you different quality goods than normal. Sometimes you also get short-changed on the quantity. For example, your restaurant orders ten dozen rolls and each dozen is short one roll.

The supplier is in need of money and is willing to sacrifice the good will and continued patronage of his customers in order to pick up some quick money.

C. It's Never Good Enough

The purchaser has developed higher standards, which were never contemplated, nor agreed upon, by the parties. Very rarely do people simply refuse to pay; they usually have a reason. Someone who always ordered cheaper products of lower quality now claims that the goods do not meet his standards. You can explain to him that he got what he paid for, but he is really looking for an excuse not to pay the full price. He cannot afford to payout and is seeking a reason not to do so. At best, from his point of view, he will be able to delay the payment and may even obtain a reduction in price.

D. A Sale Becomes A Consignment

Dresses were not sold during the season and are now being returned to you for full credit. The buyer thought that this was the agreement. He will not pay for the dresses, and the season has passed. Needless to say, he bargained you down to a cheap price before making the purchase, and he fell behind in his payments some time ago. The dresses now can only be sold at the "after-season" sales at substantial markdowns. If you do not take back the dresses, you may get nothing. It is your decision whether to take back the dresses and never again sell to him on credit, or to simply sue him, it is more of a business decision than a legal one.

E. A Customary Practice is Now Changed

The common trade practice in your industry is now being reinterpreted by one of your customers. You agree to a flat rate, only to be billed for alleged "add-ons." What was to be a fixed fee now becomes a contingency fee. The terms of payment are greatly extended. When someone radically changes his manner of doing business, it is a sign that something is wrong. The rules are being bent so that more money will be made or less will be spent. This is a danger sign.

F. A Loan Becomes An Equity investment

You advance money to help a customer, expecting prompt repayment, only to discover that you are now his partner. What you thought was a short-term loan now becomes a long-term investment. Investments such as these rarely succeed. When this happens, there usually is a lack of sufficient documentation to show the intention of a short-term loan. Obviously, the loan cannot be repaid and there is most likely insufficient cash flow available to pay interest. It is your decision whether to sue for your money or let the investment ride.

Chapter 2

WHAT YOUR LAWYER
SHOULD TELL YOU

*It is a pleasant world we live in, sir, a very
pleasant world. There are bad people in it, Mr.
Richard, but if there were no bad people, there
would be no good lawyers.*

—Charles Dickens,
The Old Curiosity Shop

Once you notice that you might be dealing with a bad-debt
scenario, you should contact an attorney. Lawyers, however,
tend to get involved with legal matters and sometimes
overlook basics. When you have to collect money, you
want more than a legal victory; you need a real victory. The
whole idea is to get the money. The role of the legal system
is to analyze the law and the facts in order to determine
which party is in the right and which is in the wrong. You,
on the other hand, are seeking to salvage the situation and
recover as much of your money as possible.

A. A Judgment Does Not Mean You Won

It's not over until it's over; meaning, it's only over when
you have the money. A Judgment is a determination that
you are due money, but does not give you any money. After
you have the Judgment, you must commence enforcement

proceedings, which may or may not be successful. If debtor has bank accounts, or other assets, you may be successful in recovering your money. At best, a Judgment is an interim step in the process of obtaining your money.

B. Business Judgment Is As Critical As Legal Knowledge

The idea is not only to win the case but also to collect the money that is due you. Unless the debtor is a total deadbeat, you should be receiving offers of settlement throughout the litigation process. Sometimes it is better to grab the money and run, while other times you may be forced to go the distance.

Someone must be in a position to decide if the defendant is good for the money in the event a Judgment is obtained. That person must be in a position where he can get a feel for the defendant's finances and sense how many other creditors are clamoring for the defendant's money. By the time you obtain the Judgment, there may not be any assets available to seize, or you may not be able to uncover any assets.

No one can be right every time and always obtain optimum results. Nevertheless, it is possible to develop skills in this area which help maximize results. Lawyers are very hesitant about making business decisions, because it is easy to be wrong and subject to criticism. Also, it is in an area that lacks absolute certainty, and most lawyers do not like to guess, when there is a chance that they can be wrong.

C. No One Can Predict the True Outcome

In this area, you are dealing with possibilities and probabilities. You know that the defendant is hurting financially, but you do not know how much he is hemorrhaging. His business may have suffered a temporary setback or a permanent collapse. Many times the debtors themselves do not know the answer. The owner of a company may be pouring his own money into a fatally ill company, believing in the bottom of his heart that it will recover and be stronger. No one really knows about any individual debtor who is having trouble.

Large consumer credit companies keep detailed and accurate records of a great number of individual debtors. Statistical prognostications may be fairly accurate in determining overall debt levels for their entire consumer portfolio. With profiles and histories, these large consumer credit companies can determine with a great deal of accuracy those with good credit risk and those who have bad credit. However, once an account goes bad, they cannot have any level of certainty as to their ability to collect what is due to them or the amount they will successfully collect. The law of large numbers applies to many cases, but at best, it is a rudimentary guide for an individual case. For that matter, the tendency of the large consumer credit companies is oftentimes to just grab the money and run.

Large commercial credit companies have even poorer prognostication abilities. When times are good, they make money, but when times are bad, they suffer serious losses. Several commercial lenders have recently undergone reorganizations due to bankruptcy from their uncollectible accounts. Both consumer and commercial lenders rely upon high interest rates to cover their loan losses. Most commercial lenders also take security interests in their borrower's receivables, equipment, or inventory to give them further protection.

D. Contingency Fees with an Attorney

Most attorneys' fees in collection cases are contingent upon the collection of money. The attorney requires a percentage of the money collected. If you collect no money, then he recovers no fee. He basically becomes your partner in the case. This is because both he and you know that there is no guarantee that any money will be collected. In the event that money is collected, no one is sure if it will be the full amount. His fee is dependent on how well you do. This is a good approach, as every time there is an offer of settlement, the attorney must give it due consideration.

It encourages the attorney to maximize the amount received, as that will maximize his fee. He can proceed to Judgment and enforcement proceedings if he feels the money is there, or he can take a settlement if he is fearful. Either way, you and he both have the same goal and will receive proportionate rewards. You do not have to worry about the attorney "running up" a bill, and you know that you share a common interest in obtaining the most money available from the debtor.

Chapter 3

RULES OF THUMB

Some people use one half their ingenuity to get into debt, and the other half to avoid paying it.

-George D. Prentice

There are several common rules that must always be considered while engaged in credit sensitive litigation. The rules set forth below are not hard and fast, but should be treated as guidelines.

A. You Are Rarely the Only Creditor

Unless the debtor has a particular disliking for you, there will be other creditors sharing your unhappiness. You must be as concerned about the other creditors as you are about the debtor. You are all fighting to grab from the same pot of money. Thus, you must guide yourself accordingly when dealing with the debtor. You must always remember that if he owes you, then he also owes others. Bear this in mind when considering deferring payments or entering into payment schedules.

If you sue, then you will grab his attention. You must make inquiries into his level of debt, to determine if by deferring payment or entering into a payment plan, you will ever receive any money. You must always try to be first in line and try to make the debtor responsive to your needs.

B. Speed Counts

Time is a meter running in favor of the debtor. He is using your money to pay other creditors and stay in business. If you wait, someone will get there first. The longer you wait, the less money will remain.

Everyone is hesitant about starting a lawsuit, because it usually ends any sense of good will with the other party. The debtor may be nice and polite to you, but if he keeps failing in his promise to pay, then you are in trouble. You grab the debtor's attention when you make him hire a lawyer.

The longer you sit on an unpaid receivable, the less likely you are to collect on that amount. You must work quickly if you are going to receive your money. You can always apologize later if you made a mistake and the debtor was simply tardy but is willing to pay. Most suspicions are usually correct, and if you have serious doubts about payment, then you will probably be correct.

Usually, serious negotiations start when the lawsuit is commenced, and continue to progress until the eve of trial or a motion for summary judgment is made. The sooner you start the case, the sooner the negotiations will progress. The court process itself takes time, and you must allow for that as well. By quickly starting the lawsuit, the debtor will recognize that you are serious about collecting your money. As the lawsuit progresses, he will realize that he is running out of time. There are other creditors competing for this money, and you want to get your fair share before it runs out.

C. Better A Fight Than A Surrender

Most clients get very excited and happy when their attorney tells them that the defendant has not answered, and he has obtained a default judgment. A default judgment is unfortunately rarely a good sign. When a defendant puts in an answer and fights the case, you know there is money to be had. If the defendant lies down and dies he was probably already dead in the first place. He does not care whether another Judgment is entered against him as there are no remaining assets to satisfy the Judgment.

Sometimes as a ploy to buy more time a defendant will allow you to enter a default Judgment and when you move to enforce it he will then obtain an Order to Show Cause to vacate the Judgment and serve his Answer. Inexperienced debtors do not take the Summons or lawsuit seriously until a Marshal comes to close them down.

If a defendant gives you a strong fight, seeking to delay the inevitable Judgment, then you should be aware that this is being used as a negotiating tool, in an effort to obtain a better settlement, or to buy time so he can continue to harbor his financial resources.

D. "Assets" Are Never Real

A company having financial problems may appear to have a strong balance sheet, but it may not be real. Neither inventory nor receivables age gracefully.

Although a financially weak company may show a large inventory, it will probably consist of goods that either are out of style or slightly damaged. Part of its inventory will consist of older products that are now obsolete, or for which there is little demand. Rest assured that those goods that are marketable have already been sold and that less desirable, but semi-marketable goods have already been sold at discount prices. The remaining inventory should most likely have been junked long ago.

It also does not mean much for an insolvent company to have high receivables. The good customers have already paid their bills. What is left over is either due and owing from customers who were dissatisfied with the goods they received or from those who do not have the money to pay.

As a company declines, it must sell to inferior customers to whom its competitors would hesitate in extending credit. Also, as the company's competitive edge declines, its products become less competitive and subject to greater customer dissatisfaction.

E. Going Concerns Should Be Kept Alive

Every effort should be made to try to keep the debtor in business and operating. Dead concerns do not generate cash, and their receivables and inventory are worth even less. No matter how much you want to bury the debtor, you must give serious consideration to keeping him living and breathing so that there may be some possibility of receiving money.

Involuntary bankruptcy should only be used to stop preferential transfers or fraudulent conveyances. If the debtor is using his remaining funds to pay his friends or to give to his family, then he should be shut down.

Everyone who feels deceived or cheated wants to inflict financial harm on the person who harmed them. No matter how tempting it is, you will not get back your money by burying the debtor. The threat is more beneficial than the reality. Sometimes it is better if the debtor is struggling to survive than out of business altogether.

F. Only Fools Are Frightened by Letters

New York businessmen are sophisticated and tough. Telephone calls and letters are not going to intimidate them. You must start a lawsuit if you are going to get their attention.

By the time a business is failing, the proprietor has had his fill of angry customers and suppliers. He has learned to accept and live with the complaints and threats. A letter from a lawyer, especially if that lawyer is in a distant city, will mean nothing and will be considered junk mail. A lawsuit forces the debtor to react and do something. He must respond or you will proceed to attach his assets. That will make him stand up and pay attention.

G. Keep Copies of Checks Received

Many people do not know the full and correct name of the entity that owes them money. They may know the names of the people they deal with or the trade name that the business goes under, but they never know their true name. Even the entity's stationery can be deceiving by only carrying an abbreviation or trade name.

Most checks carry the full legal name of the entity, and copies should be made of checks received before depositing them. Many entities actually carry out their business through multiple corporations, and the checks will bear the names of the various corporations that are making the payments. As an added bonus, you also now know where they bank, so that when you obtain a Judgment you will know where to serve the Restraining Notice and Property Execution.

It is not that people seek to deceive, but it is common for many entities to operate by their trade names rather than their legal corporate names. If is much easier to discover their true names when times are good, rather than when they are already in trouble

H. Litigation is An Alternative Form of Negotiation

War is an alternative form of diplomacy. Your goal is to collect your money with a technical legal victory being secondary. This is the carrot-and-whip approach. The litigation puts the debtor under pressure and encourages him to negotiate with you.

You want your money as soon as possible, and you want to stay ahead of the other creditors. You want to catch his attention. You want him to regard you as a threat and not just a nuisance. Do not get caught up in litigation to the extent of excluding all negotiations. In real life the overwhelming majority of cases are settled and not tried. You must keep all options open and proceed on all forms if you are going to recover your money.

I. Your Adversary Has Already prepared For The Lawsuit

You will find that most of the debtor's marketable assets are gone by the time you start the lawsuit. The debtor is more conscious of his financial situation than you are. He has been liquidating whatever he can to raise money to remain in business. He knows he owes money and needs to raise it somehow.

Rarely are debtors caught by surprise when they receive a Summons and Complaint. They might not have expected to receive it from you, but they knew someone was going to start a lawsuit against them.

In our experience, it matters little if the debtor is a privately held or public corporation. They all seem to act the same way. They will cannibalize the marketable assets to stay alive. They rarely get sued by just one creditor, and they have developed an approach to dealing with the lawsuits.

J.   Always Try to Work It Out

These matters rarely end gracefully. Be prepared to lose a client or customer. Usually some form of settlement is reached, and they almost never go down to the bitter end. Most debtors are bitter and angry about their financial plight, and this hostility will become apparent in your conversations with them.

You must be clear and level-headed, even when they are not. Every effort must be made by you to inject some rationality into the discussions.

As stated earlier, the debtor is likened to a drowning man trying to grab on to any hand, even if he has to pull the person into the water to stay alive. You have to focus on getting your money. It is up to you to keep things moving and negotiations progressing.

K. Always Use Local Counsel

You cannot do this long-distance. You must use a local attorney if you are going to achieve meaningful results. Local counsel knows the local courts and may even know of the debtor and his attorney. He is familiar with the way the local system works.

If you cannot find a local attorney, then your attorney can find one for you. The Commercial Law League of America can put you in touch with local attorneys. There are several services such as the National Law List, which publishes directories of local attorneys in each city. It is not enough to have an attorney from the same locality. You need someone who knows the courts and the key players.

Chapter 4

TYPES OF LEGAL VENUES

*Action is the foundational key to all success.
Knowing is not enough! Lots of people know what
to do, but few people actually do what they know.*

—Tony Robbins

A. Federal Court

We have two court systems in the United States-the federal
system and the state court system, because most of the cases
do not meet the jurisdictional requirements of diversity
required for federal issues. We also find that whenever we
represent a small, struggling defendant in federal court,
we tend to get a better shake than we would in the state
court. Somehow, in our experience, the federal judges and
magistrates seem more kindly disposed to honest debtors
who have fallen on bad times.

Lastly, but importantly, we have found federal court to
require much more work and effort than the state courts.
This works well for larger cases, but it generally makes
smaller cases uneconomical.

B. State Court Procedures

As practicing attorneys for more than thirty years between us in New York City, we will be writing about the courts in New York City. We will be focusing on the Civil Court system, and the state court system known as the Supreme Court. Basically, the Civil Court deals with claims for monetary damages that are below $25,000, while the Supreme Court system handles cases above $25,000 and can give equitable relief. If you need an injunction or specific performance, then you must go to the Supreme Court.

A) Civil Court

The Civil Court of the City of New York has a separate court in each of the five boroughs of New York City. These courts handle landlord tenant summary proceedings of both a residential and commercial nature, whether for non-payment or for a holdover (a violation of the lease other than the payment of rent). In landlord-tenant summary proceedings, there is no jurisdictional limit on the amount of money involved. For example, a summary proceeding for non-payment of rent can be commenced against a residential tenant who owes $750 for last month's rent, or against a commercial lessee of a large office building who owes millions of dollars.

The Civil Court also handles lawsuits to recover money for personal injuries, property damage, or for monies due and owing with a jurisdictional limit of $25,000. If you need to sue for more than $25,000, then you must bring the action in the Supreme Court of the State of New York, which also has branches in each of the boroughs.

In general, the Civil Court is cheaper and quicker than the Supreme Court. It costs $45 to buy an index number in

Civil Court, as opposed to $210 in the Supreme Court. A request for judicial intervention is $95, and a Note of Issue is $30 in Supreme Court, as opposed to $40 for a Notice of Trial in Civil Court.

More importantly, things move quicker in Civil Court, as they are geared for the more rapid disposal of cases. We find that there is substantially less motion practice and paperwork. Cases under $10,000 go to compulsory arbitration, where they are usually resolved. Either party may file for a trial de novo if they are not satisfied with the arbitrator's determination, but few do. These arbitrations take less than one hour to complete.

A whole bench trial (a trial before a Judge, without a jury) can be started and completed in a morning. One of the major reasons for the efficiency in the Civil Court is that the cases are for smaller sums of money and the attorneys are not looking to expend great amounts of effort or time. This works for the plaintiff's benefit in trying to speed its case along. Many cases originally commenced in the Supreme Court are remanded under Section 325-d to the Civil Court for trial if the court sees the actual amounts in dispute are small enough to be tried in Civil Court. In those cases, the jurisdiction of the Civil Court is raised to the amount in the Complaint.

After a Judgment is obtained in Civil Court, the plaintiff may obtain a transcript of the Judgment and docket it with the County Clerk in the Supreme Court. This gives it the same status as if it was a Judgment obtained in the Supreme Court. The main advantage is that it then becomes a lien (an obligation) upon any real property within that county. A plaintiff may then obtain a transcript from the County Clerk, and docket the transcript of the Judgment in other counties where he believes the debtor may own real Property.

Generally, we prefer bringing collection actions in Civil Court. If we have several causes of action, we might consider bringing them separately in Civil Court, rather than consolidate them into one large case in Supreme Court

B) Supreme Court

The Supreme Court of the State of New York has unlimited monetary jurisdiction and can award equitable relief. It is the highest trial court of primary jurisdiction in New York. In New York City, it is an extremely busy and active court.

The sheer volume of cases handled by the court lengthens the litigation process and can cause delays. After you have served a Summons and Complaint and the defendant has appeared, the case will be assigned to a specific Justice when there is the need for judicial intervention. When one of the parties makes a motion or requests a conference or trial, the case will be assigned to a specific Justice who will remain with the case until disposition of the case.

The court has set up a special unit with its own clerk's office and specifically assigned Justices to hear commercial cases, as opposed to the bulk of the cases, which involve property damage and personal injury, These specifically assigned justices are very knowledgeable in commercial matters and know how to move the case along while maintaining an environment conducive for settlement. Needless to say, as in most courts, almost all the cases are settled rather than tried.

In many cases, defendants counterclaim against the plaintiff, Most of these counterclaims are frivolous and are done for the sole purpose of improving their settlement posture. Counterclaims are to be expected, and they should not scare you. They are to be dealt with in the usual course of business.

There is substantial motion practice in Supreme Court. It is common for defendants to engage in motion practice in order to delay the case and tie it up in court. As a plaintiff you should be careful only to make those motions which have a strong chance of expediting the case. Motions for summary judgment should only be made when you have good documentary evidence. Motions based on Affidavits of Fact will be countered by affidavits on behalf of the defendant. Questions of fact tend to appear from the air. The court loathes granting summary judgment if there are any questions of fact. For the plaintiff it is almost always better to try to get the case to trial as quickly as possible.

The same rules apply to discovery and particularly to examinations before trial. Defendants wish to engage in lengthy discovery for the purpose of avoiding trial. Discovery procedure can also encourage motion practice, which will add further delays. A plaintiff should promptly comply with the defendant's discovery demands and promptly submit its witnesses for oral depositions, but should be very careful to limit its own discovery demands. The defendant will seek to avoid and delay responding to plaintiff's demands, and it will again engender unnecessary motion practice.

Generally, bench trials—those trials before a Justice—are more efficient and consistent than jury trials in commercial cases. Defendants will seek jury trial, but you should generally make efforts to avoid them. In commercial matters, judicial decisions will be more consistent and accurate than jury determinations.

Chapter 5

HOW TO ENFORCE YOUR MONEY JUDGMENT

I am a great believer in luck, and I find the harder I work, the more I have of it.

—Thomas Jefferson

A. Supplementary Proceedings

As we said, getting the Judgment is only one part of the process. You must then proceed to locate assets and enforce your Judgment, through supplementary proceedings. In these, you serve a Notice of Entry of Judgment notifying the debtor that the court has issued a Judgment, and starting his time to appeal. The debtor has thirty days from the receipt of the Notice of Entry of Judgment to file an appeal.

If the debtor is a natural person, you must also send him notice that certain sources of income, as well as certain assets, cannot be attached or restrained by a Judgment creditor. This note may be attached to the Notice of Entry of Judgment, with the restraining notice or sent separately,

B. Subpoenas

After you obtain a Judgment, you are permitted to serve a subpoena upon the debtor, requiring him to appear either in court or at your office, to be examined for the purpose of determining if he has assets subject to attachment. There are printed forms that even contain appropriate questions to ask the debtor in order to locate his assets.

Most debtors do not respond to subpoenas. It is usually necessary to obtain a contempt order, requiring them to appear or be held in contempt by the court. If they do not respond, you can enforce the contempt order by obtaining a billable attachment, which imposes fines or incarceration against them for failure to appear.

With this, you are entitled to the same enforcement rights as with a regular subpoena. While answering in writing is not the same as orally examining a debtor there is a higher chance of compliance, and it usually provides the basic information necessary to proceed with your investigation.

You do not require a process server to serve an information subpoena, nor do you have to schedule a specific date to examine its recipient. Because of this, you can serve such a subpoena at modest cost upon a wider variety of individuals and entities, Needless to say, except for financial institutions, there is still a low rate of compliance, and most responses provide minimal levels of information.

Information subpoenas are usually served with restraining notices, stopping any person or institution from releasing the debtor's funds in its possession.

We find that subpoenas are expensive and time-consuming, and should only be used in large cases. Usually, they provide very little information, and the debtor is often well-prepared against them. While it can be used as an approach to facilitate negotiations, it usually does not pay. In our experience, subpoenas and contempt proceedings are mostly used to pressure debtors and do not tend to accomplish much more.

C. Information Subpoenas

An information subpoena is an alternative to a regular subpoena. It is served by certified mail and contains an annexed questionnaire for the debtor or any third party. You can purchase such questionnaires at legal stationery supply stores for individuals, corporations, and financial institutions.

D. Investigators

Based on our experience, we find that supplementary proceedings are not very productive. Sometimes you get lucky, but it is not common. We firmly recommend the use of a good investigator. It is well worth it.

Investigators do not wear trench coats and lurk in shadows. They rarely leave their offices. Most work today is done while sitting at a computer, searching databases. The more information you give the investigator the better his results will be. Some basic information that can help an investigator includes: full name, social security number, residence, place of business, and bank. While you may not have all this information, having some will certainly aid in the search.

Saved copies of any checks you received from the debtor provide a plethora of information (e.g., the debtor's full name, and the name of the bank, which he may even still be using). Investigators can provide you with the names of possible financial institutions upon which to serve restraining notices and information subpoenas.

E. Enforcement Proceedings

Enforcement proceedings are used to collect the money awarded to you in the Judgment. They operate independently from supplementary proceedings, although they can work either simultaneously or in tandem.

F. Restraining Notices

Serving a restraining notice is usually the first step, as it is easy and cheap. It is a simple form, obtained from any stationery store, served on both the debtor and on third parties (people holding assets of the debtor or people who owe money to the debtor).

The restraining notice informs its recipient to hold on to any money they have belonging to the debtor and not to give it to him. You can serve a restraining notice on a bank where the debtor has his money. The bank will be restrained from paying out money from the account. If the debtor has written checks from that account to pay his bills, then those checks will "bounce" and will not be honored by the debtor's bank.

Restraining notices can be served by certified mail. It is not uncommon to mail them to all banks in the neighborhood where the debtor resides or maintains a place of business. You need not serve a restraining notice on each branch of the same bank. A restraining notice served on the bank will restrain all bank accounts of the debtor, irrespective of the branch. It is not possible to serve a restraining notice on a bank that is not in the same state as the Judgment. All a restraining notice does is "restrain" money that belongs to the debtor. Proceedings may be brought to recover monies that are paid out over a restraining notice. In practice, debtors never honor restrained monies. The notices are served for the purposes of putting the debtor on notice that collectors are coming, so that negotiations may be encouraged. Proceedings to enforce notices are rarely seen. Restraining notices are always honored by financial institutions. Many times, there is a delay in processing the restraining notice and the debtor may be able to remove his funds from the account before the bank can implement the freezing of the account.

Restraining notices are commonly served with information subpoenas so that when you hit a live bank account, the bank will inform you as to how much money has been restrained, as well as the nature of the funds.

If the debtor is a landlord, restraining notices should be served on his tenants. If the debtor is a supplier, then the restraining notices should be served on his customers. The restraining notices, so served, will only be honored by those customers and other people who want an excuse not to pay the debtor.

G. Income Executions

Income executions can only be used to garnish an individual debtor's salary. An income execution is served by a City Marshal or a Sheriff, first at the employee's home and then at his place of employment. You can obtain a maximum of 10 percent of the debtor's salary.

Income executions are primarily used on consumer claims, where the debtor has failed to pay his credit cards and his salary is now being garnished to pay the Judgment obtained by the credit card company. It is a long, slow process that works for smaller sums of money.

H. Property Executions

Property executions are used to seize assets of the debtor. A property execution is served by a City Marshal or Sheriff on the debtor, or on any entity holding assets of the debtor. After you have received a response to your information subpoena and restrained the bank account, the Marshal or Sheriff then proceeds to execute on the account and seize the money within it.

A property execution can also be served on the debtor's place of business. If the debtor does not pay the monies due and owing, then the Marshal or Sheriff will inventory the assets and schedule a sale. The Marshal or Sheriff is empowered to sell off the debtor's assets to satisfy the Judgment. Usually, a fraction of the true value of the assets is realized at a Marshal's or Sheriff's sale. The sale is a means of last resort. It is basically a way of putting the debtor out of business, or, more realistically, threatening to do so.

I. Turnover Proceedings

Sometimes you will find the debtor's assets and they are not entirely in his name alone. The most common example is a joint bank account. In those cases, you must commence special proceedings to have the debtor's share of the assets turned over to you. These proceeding can be brought in any county where you have located the asset, and need not be brought in the same court where you obtained your Judgment. For example, you may have obtained a Judgment in Brooklyn but located a joint bank account in Nassau County. Provided you have docketed a transcript of the Judgment in Nassau, you should bring the turnover proceeding in Nassau, where the bank account is located.

J.   City Marshal or Sheriff

In enforcing a Judgment, whether by property or income execution, there is a decision to be made as to who should enforce it. A Judgment may only by enforced by a City Marshal or Sheriff.

A Sheriff, or Deputy Sheriff, is a governmental employee of the State of New York, and all its employees are state municipal workers. A City Marshal is appointed by the City to perform these services, but is self-employed, using his own staff and facilities. The statutory fees you pay are the same for both.

It has been our experience that you are always better off with a City Marshal who is self-employed and more entrepreneurial in outlook. The City Marshal can only make money if he works, he cannot rely on a salary. Most lawyers establish working relationships with a particular Marshal so that there can be open and honest dialogue as to approaches to collection. They can weigh together any offers of settlement or payout schedules. You can also get a feel from the Marshal as to the viability of debtor's business.

In addition to a small fee, which is seventy dollars (fifty-five dollars if bank levy) for a Property Execution, the Marshal or Sheriff receives a poundage fee of 5 percent of all funds collected.

Chapter 6

SECURITY INTERESTS

'Tis against some men's principle to pay interest, and seems against others' interest to pay the principle.

—Benjamin Franklin

A popular means of obtaining some protection on a loan is to obtain a perfected security interest in the debtor's personal property. Personal property is anything other than real estate, and includes inventory, fixtures, receivables, equipment, and furnishings. It can also include paper assets, such as stocks, bonds, artwork, and bank accounts.

A. Types of Security Interest

1. *"True" legal mortgage*

A legal mortgage occurs when assets are transferred to the secured party as security for an obligation, but subject to the right to have the assets returned to the obligor when the obligations are performed.

2. *Equitable mortgage*

A deed conveying real property, which, by any other written instrument, appears to be intended only as a security in the nature of a mortgage, although an absolute conveyance in terms, must be considered a mortgage; and the person for whose benefit such deed is made, derives no advantage from the recording thereof, unless every writing, operating as a defeasance of the same, or explanatory of its being desired to have the effect only of a mortgage, or conditional deed, is also recorded therewith, and at the same time.

3. Statutory mortgage

There are some jurisdictions which allow assets to be mortgaged without a transference of title. Primarily, statutory mortgages associated to land, registered aircraft and registered ships.

4. Equitable charge

An equitable charge is when debtor retains control and use of the asset, and the creditor has a claim on that asset in the event that a default on the obligation should take place. Typically with this arrangement, the creditor has the right to make use of the judicial process to petition for, and secure ownership of, the asset as a means of settling the defaulted debt. An equitable charge does not pass on the ownership, title or possession to a creditor but gives him or her the right to the judicial process for recovery of the loan amount in case of non-payment.

5. Floating charge

A floating charge is a security interest where the asset can change in quantity and/or value from time to time (for example inventory). If debtor defaults, the floating asset 'freezes' and the floating charge becomes a fixed charge making the lender a priority creditor.

6. Pledge

A Pledge is where the underlying asset that is being pledged is physically delivered to creditor.

7. Legal lien

A lien is an encumbrance on the debtor's property to secure the debt.

8. Equitable lien

An equitable lien is a type of security interest where a court imposes the lien on the property in order to achieve fairness, mainly when someone has possession of property that he or she holds for another.

9. Hypothecation

Hypothecation is when a debtor pledges an asset, while keeping ownership and the benefits of the asset. With hypothecation, the creditor has the right to seize the asset if the debtor cannot pay the debit as stipulated.

10. Conditional sale

Conditional sale is when the debtor retains title to the asset, but the item is given to the creditor; sometimes called an executory contract.

B. Security Interests On Personal Property

It is easy and cheap to accomplish a security interest, as all you need is a security agreement and the filing of a Uniform Commercial Code form (UCC-1) financial statement. The security agreement states the nature of the security interest, its terms, and conditions. The UCC-1 financing statement puts all third parties and the general public on notice.

Co-operative apartments are considered personality, and all co-op loans are held by a security interest on the proprietary lease and stock certificate. A security interest on negotiable instruments is only perfected by actual possession of the installment and it is for that reason that the bank takes physical possession of the stock certificate and proprietary lease, which together constitute the ownership of your apartment.

Security agreements and the filing of UCC-1 financing statement are also commonly used in the sale of a business or restaurant where the seller gives purchase money financing to the purchaser. Traditionally in such a sale, twenty-five percent will be paid in cash at the closing, with the seller financing the remaining seventy-five percent, which will be paid off with interest over time. The security interest will cover all the furniture, equipment, inventory, and fixtures at the place of business.

Security interests are not perfect and can be difficult to enforce. If you are holding precious jewelry, valuable art, or securities in your actual physical possession, then it is easier to enforce your rights. If you want to stop innocent third parties from purchasing assets, which are security for your loan, then the UCC-1 financing statement will give you protection. Seizing assets from a difficult debtor is another story.

You basically need peaceable entry if you are going to enter a store, warehouse, or restaurant and seize your security. Usually, you make a deal with the debtor and pay him some money to take back your assets. Many assets have little value when they are removed from their present location. A fully furnished and operating restaurant has value, but if you have to sell the individual chairs, tables, china, and cooking equipment, then you suffer a tremendous decline in sale value. Usually you must pay a little for peaceable entry if you are going to recover the value of your security.

The exception to this is the replevin proceeding to recover automobiles when the owner has failed to make his lease or car loan payments. The financing of cars is the most common secured consumer lending procedure in the United States. Because of these, procedures have been developed for the rapid seizing of cars where the owner has defaulted in his obligation.

C. Security interests on Real Property

A security interest in real property is called a mortgage. When someone borrows money on real estate, he signs a note, which is the obligation to make payments and pay interest, and a mortgage, which is the security to pay. These may also be a UCC-1 financing statement to cover personal property in the building.

A mortgage foreclosure proceeding is expensive and lengthy. You can stop the debtor from collecting rent by having a Receiver appointed by the court. Very few receivers manage buildings well, and their fees and legal costs eat up all the income.

It is possible to arrange with the mortgagor (the debtor) for you to obtain a deed in lieu of foreclosure, by paying him some money and having him simply deed the property back to you.

In general, the major advantage of a UCC-1 financing statement or of a mortgage is that it gives you a priority over unsecured lenders and it puts the world on notice of your lien, so that the debtor cannot dispose of this asset to third parties without them having legal knowledge of your rights and interests.

Chapter 7

RATIONALIZATION OF ACCOUNTS PAYABLE

Courage is simply the willingness to be afraid and act anyway.

—Robert Anthony

Many debtors understand their problems and know their financial condition. They want to avoid bankruptcy and also maintain their livelihood.

The rationalization of accounts payable is a term for, what in reality is an informal reorganization. The debtor contacts his creditors and offers to settle his debts at a substantial discount, which can range from seventy-five percent to as low as five percent of the amount due.

It usually starts with the debtor or his attorney sending a letter to each of the creditors, telling them about the debtor's adverse financial situation and sometimes enclosing a copy of the debtor's balance sheet and income-and-expense statement. The letter will offer to settle the debtor's claims at a discounted price, with payments to be made immediately or over time. Usually, unless the debtor is very cunning, the same identical letter is sent to each creditor.

The information disclosure is usually real and deceptive. The financial statements will not properly reflect non-cash asset values, or will indicate an improving condition.

Any financial statements submitted by the debtor are usually out of date and do not reflect the debtor's current situation. It could be that there has been a pickup in sales, new customers, or that a product has become successful. You will never really know, and they will never tell you the absolute truth. It could also be that the debtor is simply trying to avoid bankruptcy.

The source of the debtor's funds is also always murky and unclear. It could be a bank loan, other assets, or real property shown for the purpose of consolidating debts. The funds can also come from an infusion of money from existing shareholders, or from a new investor seeking to save money. Again, you will never really know, and they will not tell you. The funds could come from a potential purchaser or from someone who has already bought the business and is already locked into a bad situation.

There are several reasons why a debtor will seek to pay off his loans and obligations at a discounted price. Needless to say, the primary reason is to avoid bankruptcy. The debtor cannot pay off all his loans in full, but can pay them off at a discounted price.

The debtor may already be in serious negotiations with a purchaser or investment group, and needs to improve his financial position in order to finalize the transaction. The debtor will have more appeal to outside investors if he can show its trade payables are under control and that he can continue as an operating entity without the need for a massive infusion of cash.

The debtor may be aware of an impending windfall from a large contract, successful litigation, or new product development. Thus, he wishes to be able to retain more of the money, rather than have to distribute it to its creditors. Once it becomes public knowledge, the creditors, will want all their money with interest.

In spite of all we have said, most creditors take the money and run. Some will bargain for a little more, but everyone takes the money. The rationale is fairly simple-no one likes to gamble with the unknown, especially if it has not been good up to now. The debtor has already fallen substantially behind in paying his bills. His credit history has not been satisfactory. No one really knows what the future holds. The creditor prefers having the money in his pocket, as opposed to the money being with the debtor while he awaits a positive turn of events. Basically, it is better to be safe than sorry.

It should be noted that, even in retail credit cases involving individual debtors attempting to clean up their credit, most banks will grab the money, rather than await payment in full.

Chapter 8

STRATEGIES FOR SUCCESS

A successful man is one who can lay a firm foundation with the bricks others have thrown at him.

—David Brinkley

The following is a series of approaches that must be taken and considered in dealing with debtors. No strategy is all-inclusive, but rather bits and pieces of each approach should be applied to each individual case.

A. Knowledge is Power

You must gather as much information as possible. It is usually too late when the lawyer has to do it. You should maintain in your files photocopies of all checks received that differ in name or bank from prior checks. Letterheads are also helpful. The more you know about a debtor's business, the better your chance of some success.

Do you think it is easier if a company is publicly traded? If they are in poor financial shape, then their public filings will probably be outdated. Even if their filings are current, the paperwork may not fully reflect their rapidly deteriorating condition. Even public companies know the advantages of having out-of-state bank accounts that can be attached in the event of a Judgment in the same state as the bank.

You must rely upon investigators if you are going to obtain useful information on the debtor. You can also search the internet for Web sites or blogs posted by employees of the debtor. Supplementary proceedings are cumbersome and take time. You are competing against other creditors and you must locate assets before they do.

B. Business Decisions

We cannot stress enough how astute business decisions must be made in conjunction with pragmatic legal advice. You are in the case to collect money, not to obtain landmark judicial determinations. In almost all cases, there exists negotiation and posturing. The important decision is how much to settle for and when to do it. There are no hard-and-fast rules, and all involve practical business decisions. Settlement always involves risk and uncertainty, as you never know if you left anything on the table, or if it would have been wiser to settle than to chase a debtor after Judgment.

C. Good Cop—Bad Cop

Lines of communication must always remain open if there will be any possibility of settlement. In working with debtors, there should always be one person, whether the attorney or the client, who keeps the negotiations going. It is the role of one of the parties to let the debtor know that the case is being pursued. It is critical that each one understands his or her role and is able to communicate to each other, accurately, how matters are progressing.

D. Payment Over Time

In trying to settle these matters, you will have the dilemma as to whether to take a small sum up front or a large sum over time. This is not about the time value of money, but about your tolerance for risk. Are you really prepared to wait for your money knowing that they may soon be out of business?

There are several approaches to this issue. You can negotiate for a large payment over time, and then offer the debtor a large discount if he pays it off sooner. The payment over time offer gives you a handle in negotiating a lump-sum payment.

In considering accepting payments over time, you should factor in how long you can realistically expect to receive payments. Even if you enter into a three- or five-year payout, if you expect them to remain in business for more than one year, then you accept the payout rather than take 10 percent of the amount due.

Even while receiving payments, you can always offer a substantial discount for a lump-sum payment of the amounts due.

E. Seeking Other Creditors

It greatly helps not to be alone in the dark, and it is usually mutually beneficial if you can trade notes with other creditors. The debtor may have told you one story, but has told a different tale to others, Also, small pieces of information can add up and give everyone a clearer picture.

You find creditors able to exchange information when they all know each other or are all in the same industry as the debtor. Remember, if he owes you money, he probably owes money to your competitors. Knowing how much money is owed to each collector may give you a more realistic picture of the debtor's problem, and help everyone in negotiations. The debtor does not need to know that you are communicating with other creditors.

F. Bankruptcy

Bankruptcy is something you want the debtor to avoid. There are two primary kinds of bankruptcy: straight bankruptcy (known as Chapter 7), which is a liquidation and sale of the debtor's assets; and reorganization (known as Chapter 11), which is an attempt to rehabilitate the debtor and compromise his debts so he can remain in business. Neither one works very well for creditors.

In a straight liquidation bankruptcy, assets are sold at a fire sale, and the tax authorities receive the first monies. Old inventory, used equipment, and furniture do not tend to sell for much. Neither creditors nor debtors benefit from this. It is simply a way of ending a business. Most companies that try to reorganize do not succeed in doing so. It is rare that a company that emerges from bankruptcy court is able to continue its business.

Any three creditors can place a debtor in involuntary bankruptcy. You should only do this if you are fearful or have knowledge of preferential transfers of fraudulent conveyances. A preferential transfer exists when the debtor is paying off other creditors but is not paying you. He is using his remaining funds to pay off his friends, so that when he goes back into business, they will ship him goods. The purpose of bankruptcy is for the equal distribution of funds to all creditors. In that case, you should put the debtor in bankruptcy so that you get your fair share of the funds.

some would stop. If the stakes went to twenty dollars a flip, then most would drop out. However, if we offered to flip the coin for twenty dollars but offered 2-1 odds rather than even odds, most would still play because of the advantage.

If I raised the stakes to one hundred dollars, many would refuse to play even at 2-1 odds. If I raised the odds to 5-1, then most would play because of the overwhelming odds in their favor. Again, if I raise the stakes to one thousand dollars, even if I were to offer 10-1 odds, most would refuse to play despite the possible payout of ten thousand dollars a throw. In speaking with an attorney, you can use this little test to determine his and your own relative level of risk tolerance.

Chapter 9

ASSET PROTECTION TRUSTS

As I get older, my sense of humor is my biggest
asset.

—David Alan Grier

We live in a litigious society and a world where more people are prone to take financial risk. No one wants to be a defendant or a debtor, and most people are fearful of falling into that position. Many people are seeking to protect their assets before they become at risk. All this has led to the development of the Asset Protection Trust ("APT").

A. Asset Protection Trust ("APT")

Historically, the APT developed from what used to be called the sprinkling trust (or spendthrift trust). Under this kind of trust, the trustee was empowered to pay out income as well as principal to any or all of the individuals named as beneficiaries under the trust. A trust might be set up by parents for their three children, with the trustee empowered to pay out the income or principal of the trust as he desires. If two children were investment bankers and the third a social worker, the trustee might be inclined to give a greater share to the social worker, as he probably had a great need for the funds. Likewise, if two children were solid citizens and the third a drifter, the trustee would likely pay the money to only two of the children.

The foreign APT is a different version of the sprinkling trust. Originally, many small countries successfully established a substantial financial business by becoming "tax havens." This industry came under strong attack by our government, because it was causing a serious decline in tax revenues. Looking for another financial business, they discovered the APT.

Modern legislation for the APT was first developed in Bermuda and the Bahamas. These governments passed a set of simple statutes, which provided that there was a presumption that a conveyance made without consideration would be presumed not to be a fraudulent conveyance if it was made two years before the transferor was exposed to liability. Attorneys would not be allowed to represent parties for contingency fees, and the courts could award legal fees to the winning party. Any lawsuit to attach an asset in their country would have to be brought in a court of law in their jurisdiction.

This means you can set up a trust naming a class of beneficiaries to whom the trustee has authority to pay out the income and principal of the trust at his or her discretion. If you obey the law for two years after the trust has been set up, then there is a presumption that the trust was not intended to defraud creditors. If anyone wants to set aside this trust, then they must sue in the jurisdiction where the trust is located, such as in the Bermuda or Bahamas. Also, anyone wanting to set aside such a trust cannot hire a lawyer on a contingency fee basis, which would be based upon whether the lawyer succeeds or not, and if anyone wanting to set aside such a trust loses, they would have to pay the legal fees to the defending party of the trust.

The two-year limitation was chosen to comply with the New York Debtor and Creditor Law, so that it would be reasonable and given recognition by other foreign jurisdictions. Generally, you cannot start a successful lawsuit alleging that the foreign statute is unreasonable and intended to deceive creditors when it is similar to the law in New York and most jurisdictions.

These trusts are set up as tax-neutral because the beneficiaries of the trust report their income from the trust on their tax returns and pay full taxes on it. The foreign jurisdiction is not used as a tax haven. Under their laws, the trustee has sole discretion. The trustee also has authority to recognize any recommendations you may make about distributions of trust assets, but the trustee is not bound to honor these recommendations. Although the trustee must be in the jurisdiction, the actual assets (stocks and bonds) may be held elsewhere and may be managed by another entity. For example, the Bank of Bermuda can be the trustee, but the portfolio can be held by Citigroup or Goldman Sachs, who manages it.

You cannot set up an APT when you have already set yourself at risk and are subject to litigation. You cannot set up these trusts when you are a schoolteacher, and the next day you become a commodities trader. These trusts must be set up when you are totally clean and remain so for the next two years.

Many of these trusts were originally set up in Florida for medical doctors. In New York, if a doctor wanted hospital privileges, they would have to show the hospital that they carried 2 or 3 million dollars of malpractice insurance, while in Florida the doctor needed only to post a $25,000 bond. Many doctors would post the bond but not carry malpractice insurance, because the cost of the insurance would have a dramatic effect in reducing their income. As they prospered and in time inherited money from their parents, they developed assets. To protect these assets, but not carry malpractice insurance, they would set up an APT,

When sued, they would defend the lawsuit but also point out to the plaintiff's counsel that all their assets were in an APT and that their home was protected in bankruptcy under the strong homestead exemption that exists in Florida. This normally led to a quick and inexpensive settlement of the case.

APTs have become so popular that several states such as Delaware, South Dakota, and Alaska have established similar legislation. For example, a Delaware APT can be structured so that assets are protected from the reach of creditors, even with the trust's creator retaining an interest in the trust. A Delaware APT provides the freedom to include higher-risk assets if the trustee determines that such securities would help meet the trust's overall investment objective, and also provides that a trust does not have to pay Delaware income or capital gains taxes when there are no Delaware beneficiaries. Similarly, nonresident beneficiaries do not pay state tax on trust income or gains. Delaware does have a four-year look-back period before the presumption of not intending to defraud creditors will apply.

The use of Asset Protection Trusts is growing, and you must be aware of them, because they will affect your ability to deal with debtors.

B. How To Attack An Asset Protection Trust

There are really only three ways to attack an asset protection trust:

(1) by proving that the transfers to the trust were fraudulent transfers,

(2) by attacking the asset protection trust by using the laws of a state or jurisdiction that doesn't recognize self-settled trusts, or

(3) piercing the trust, veil piercing, alter-ego, constructive trust, or the sham transaction theory.

An individual will be deemed to be the alter ego of a corporation when:

1) The individual completely dominates and controls the finances, policy and business practice of the other corporation.
2) Such control was for an improper purpose such as "fraud or wrong, or . . . unjust act in contravention of [a third parties] legal rights."
3) The alter ego's control of the corporation caused injury to the third party.

Chapter 10

FORMS

It isn't necessary to imagine the world ending in fire or ice. There are two other possibilities: one is paperwork, and the other is nostalgia.

—Frank Zappa

The following is a list of forms used in the New York City Civil Court, New York State Supreme Court, and in supplementary proceedings.

Included also are sample legal forms that are used for some of the most common procedures in debt collection, These legal forms are included solely to make some of the debt-collection techniques discussed in this book tangible to the reader, and it is not intended that these forms should be used. This book is not to be considered legal advice, and is meant for general information purposes only. This book is not a substitute for the advice of legal counsel.

A. Civil Court Forms

1. Notice Of Entry Affidavit Of Service Of Judgment With Notice Of Entry

Entry of judgment is the final order entered by the court in the case, leaving no further action to be taken by the court with respect to the issues contested by the parties to the lawsuit. Once the judgment is entered, the winner should serve a copy of the judgment with "notice of entry" on the loser. This service starts the loser's time to appeal running

B. Service of Summons

2. Affidavit Of Service By Mail

3. Affidavit Of Service Of Order To Show Cause And Affidavit In Support

An Order to Show Cause is a way to present to a judge the reasons why the court should order relief to a party.

4. Affidavit of Service of Summons with Endorsed Complaint (Personal Delivery)

After obtaining the summons and complaint from the clerk, the litigant must then have the summons and complaint served on the other side.

Personal delivery: A copy of the summons and complaint may be served by giving it to the defendant in his or her hand.

5. Affidavit of Service of Summons with Endorsed Complaint (Other than Personal Delivery)

Substituted delivery: A copy of the summons and complaint may be left with a person other than the defendant "of suitable age and discretion" at the defendant's residence or place of business. A copy of the summons and complaint must be mailed to the defendant in an envelope marked "Personal and Confidential" within 20 days of the service on the substituted person. The envelope may not indicate that it is from an attorney or that it concerns an action against the defendant.

C. Subpoenas

6. Affidavit of Service of Subpoena to Testify

If you are unable to get a witness to appear voluntarily, or you need records produced in court that are not in your possession, you can ask the court to issue a subpoena. A subpoena is a legal document that commands the person named in it to appear in court to testify or to produce records.

7. Affidavit of Service of Subpoena for Records

D. Stipulations

8. Stipulation to Adjourn

9. Stipulation of Settlement and Affidavit Upon Default

E. Preliminary Conferences

10. Preliminary Conferences

11. Preliminary Conference Stipulation and Order For Discovery

12. Compliance Stipulation and Order

Civil Court of the City of New York

County of _____   Index Number _____

_____

                    Plaintiff(s),   **NOTICE OF ENTRY**

   -against-

_____

                    Defendant(s),

          Please take notice that the within is a true copy of a(n)

DECISION ORDER JUDGMENT duly entered in the office of the Clerk of the Civil Court of
            (choose one)

the City of New York, County of New York, on the _____ day of _____ 20____

Dated: _____

                              Signature: x _____

                              Print Name: _____

                              Address: _____

                                       _____

CIV-GP-105(12/03)i

Civil Court of the City of New York

County of _____

Index Number _____

_____

Plaintiff(s),

-against-

**AFFIDAVIT OF SERVICE
OF JUDGMENT WITH
NOTICE OF ENTRY**

_____

Defendant(s),

State of New York

County of _____ ~ss:

_____, being duly sworn, deposes and says:
(Print Name of Deponent)

1) I am over the age of 18 and not a party to this action.

2) On the _____ day of _____ 20____ I served a copy of the attached Judgment

with Notice of Entry on:

_____
(Name)

by putting it in a stamped envelope and mailing it to:

_____
(Address)

_____
(City, State, Zip)

_____
(Signature of Deponent)

Sworn to before me this _____ day
of _____ 20____

_____
(Notary Public)

CIV-GP-106(12/03)i

FREE CIVIL COURT FORM
No fee may be charged to fill in this form.
Form can be found at: https://www.nycourts.gov/courts/nyc/civil/forms.shtml.

CIVIL COURT OF THE CITY OF NEW YORK
COUNTY OF _____ : PART _____

Index No.: _____

_____
                                    Petitioner,

**AFFIDAVIT OF SERVICE
BY MAIL**

-against-

_____
                                    Respondent.

STATE OF NEW YORK
COUNTY OF _____ ss:

_____ being duly sworn,
deposes and says:

I am over 18 years of age and not a party to this action. On _____

I served _____

upon _____, the _____ in this

proceeding, by mailing a true copy of the attached papers, enclosed and properly sealed in a

postpaid envelope, which I deposited in an official depository under the exclusive care and

custody of the United States Postal Services within the State of New York addressed to

_____ the _____

at: _____

Signature: _____

Sworn to before me this _____ day of _____ 20____

_____
Notary Public or Court Employee

CIV-GP-11 (March 2001)

CIVIL COURT OF THE CITY OF NEW YORK

County of _____

        Part

Index No.: _____

_____

_____

        Claimant(s)/Plaintiff(s),

  -against-

AFFIDAVIT OF SERVICE
OF
ORDER TO SHOW CAUSE
AND
AFFIDAVIT IN SUPPORT

_____

        Defendant(s)

_____

State of New York, County of _____ ss:

_____, being duly sworn, deposes and says:

      (Name of Deponent)

I am over 18 years of age and not a party to this action. At _____ AM/PM, on _____

                                 (Time)   (Date)

at _____

                  (Address)

in the County of _____, City of New York, I served the annexed ORDER TO SHOW
CAUSE and AFFIDAVIT IN SUPPORT of the Order in this matter on:

1. _____

     (Name of Person Served)

known to me to be the _____ by:

                     (Claimant/Plaintiff/Defendant)

 ☐ (a) Delivering a true copy to him/her at the above address.

Description of Individual Served in Person:		
Sex: _____	Color of Skin: _____	Color of Hair: _____
Approximate Age: _____	Approximate Weight: _____	Approximate Height: _____

 ☐ (b) Mailing a true copy, properly sealed and enclosed in a post-paid wrapper, by Certified
     Mail, Return Receipt Requested, in a Post Office of the United States Postal Service
     within the State of New York addressed to the _____

                                   (Claimant/Plaintiff/Defendant)

           AND ALSO SERVED THEM ON

2. Marshal _____ by:

 ☐ (a) Delivering a true copy to _____

                            (Name of Person Served)

   a person in the Marshal's office.

Description of Individual Served in Person:		
Sex: _____	Color of Skin: _____	Color of Hair: _____
Approximate Age: _____	Approximate Weight: _____	Approximate Height: _____

 ☐ (b) Mailing a true copy, properly sealed and enclosed in a post-paid wrapper, by Certified
     Mail, Return Receipt Requested, in a Post Office of the United States Postal Service
     within the State of New York addressed to the above-named Marshal at:

Sworn to before me this _____ day of _____ 20.____

_____   _____

(Notary Public or Court Employee and Title)   (Signature of Deponent)

CIV-GP-19(Revised, January, 2004)-i

          FREE CIVIL COURT FORM
        No fee may be charged to fill in this form.
    Form can be found at: http://www.nycourts.gov/courts/nyc/civil/forms.shtml.

CIVIL COURT OF THE CITY OF NEW YORK
County of _____
_____
          Part

_____

_____
                         Plaintiff(s)
   -against-

_____
                        Defendant(s)

Index No. _____

**AFFIDAVIT OF SERVICE
OF SUMMONS WITH
ENDORSED COMPLAINT**
(Personal Delivery)

State of New York, County of _____ *ss:*

_____, being duly sworn, deposes and says:
         (Name of Server)
I am over 18 years of age and not a party to this action.

At _____ AM/PM, on _____ at _____
   (Time)   *(Date)*   *(Address)*
in the County of _____, City of New York, I served the attached
         (Name of County)
SUMMONS WITH ENDORSED COMPLAINT in this matter on _____
                               (Name of Defendant as shown above)
by delivering the said SUMMONS to:

_____
(Name of actual person with whom the SUMMONS was left)
☐ the said defendant in person,
   or
☐ known to me to be the _____ of the _____
                     (Title)   *(Corporation/Partnership)*

Description of Individual Served in Person:		
Sex: _____	Color of Skin: _____	Color of Hair: _____
Approximate Age: _____	Approximate Weight: _____	Approximate Height: _____

Sworn to before me this ____ day of _____ 20___

_____
(Notary Public or Court Employee and Title)

_____
(Signature of Deponent)

CIV-GP- 1 8-1 (Revised 5/04)

FREE CIVIL COURT FORM
No fee may be charged to fill in this form.
Form can be found at: https://www.nycourts.gov/courts/nyc/civil/forms.shtml.

CIVIL COURT OF THE CITY OF NEW YORK

Index No. _____

COUNTY OF _____
_____ Part
_____
_____

Plaintiff(s),

against

**AFFIDAVIT OF SERVICE
OF SUMMONS WITH
ENDORSED COMPLAINT**
(Other than Personal Delivery)

_____

Defendant(s).

_____

State of New York, County of _____ *ss:*

_____, being duly sworn, deposes and says:
Name of Server

I am over 18 years of age and not a party to this action.

At _____ AM/PM, on _____ at _____
 Time   *Date*   *Address*

in the County of _____, City of New York, I served the attached

SUMMONS WITH ENDORSED COMPLAINT in this matter on _____ by:
                                                                  Name of Defendant as shown above

☐ a) delivering the said SUMMONS to: _____
who was substituted for the defendant.   *Name of person served*

Description of Individual Substituted:
Sex:_____   Color of Skin:_____   Color of Hair:_____
Approximate Age: _____   Approximate Weight:_____   Approximate Height: _____

☐ b) affixing the summons to a conspicuous part of the door of _____
                                                                         Address

Previous attempts were made on _____

A copy of the summons and complaint was mailed to the defendant in an envelope marked
personal and confidential on _____

_____

Signature of Deponent

Sworn to before me this _____ day of _____ 20___

_____

Notary Public

CIV-GP-18A-i(5/04)

FREE CIVIL COURT FORM
No fee may be charged to fill in this form.
Form can be found at: http://www.nycourts.gov/courts/nyc/civil/forms.shtml

Civil Court of the City of New York

County of _____

_____**Part**_____

Index Number_____

Claimant(s)/Plaintiff(s)/Petitioner(s)

**AFFIDAVIT OF SERVICE
OF A SUBPOENA TO
TESTIFY**

-against-

_____*Defendant(s)/Respondent(s)*_____

State of New York, County of _____ ss.:

_____, being duly sworn, deposes and says:
(Name of person who served the papers)

I am over 18 years of age and not a party to this action. At _____ AM/PM,
(Time)

on_____ at _____
(Date) *(Address)*

in the County of _____, City of New York, I served a Subpoena
(County)

in this matter on _____ whom I know to
(Name of the witness)

to be the person named in this subpoena by delivering and leaving with him/her personally a true copy

of it and paying him/her the sum of $_____ for one day's attendance and fees for traveling to
(Amount of Fee)

the place where s/he was required by the Subpoena to attend, if required:

Description of Individual Served in Person		
Gender:_____	Color of Skin: _____	Color of Hair:_____
Approximate Age:_____	Approximate Weight:_____	Approximate Height:_____

Sworn to before me this _____ day of _____, 20____

_____
Signature of Notary Public

_____
Signature of Server

General Instructions

Anyone NOT A PARTY to the action who is over the age of 18 may serve the Subpoena.

1. Find the person to be served (the witness).
2. Give that person a copy of the Subpoena and the witness fee.
3. Give all the affidavits of service to the person on whose behalf this subpoena was
served for further proceedings in case the witness does not comply with the subpoena.

FREE CIVIL COURT FORM
No fee may be charged to fill in this form
CIV-GP-71(Reverse) (Revised 7/09)

CIVIL COURT OF THE CITY OF NEW YORK

County of _____

_____ Part

Index No.: _____

Claimant(s)/Plaintiff(s)/Petitioner(s)

-against-

**AFFIDAVIT OF SERVICE
OF
SUBPOENA FOR RECORDS**

Defendant(s)/Respondent(s)

_____

State of New York, County of _____ ss:

_____, being duly sworn, deposes and says:

(Name of person who served the papers)

I am over 18 years of age and not a party to this action. At _____ AM/PM, on

_____

(Time)   *(Date)*

at _____

_____

(Address)

in the County of _____, City of New York, I served the within Subpoena for Records in

this matter on _____ known to me to be

the Witness by: 1. delivering and leaving with him/her personally a true copy thereof;

Description of Individual Served in Person		
Gender:_____	Color of Skin:_____	Color of Hair:_____
Approximate Age:_____	Approximate Weight:_____	Approximate Height:_____

2. and paying him/her the sum of $_____ as fees for traveling to and from the place

(Amount paid)

where s/he was required by the Subpoena to attend, and for one day's attendance.

Sworn to before me this _____ day of _____, 20____

_____
Signature of Notary Public

_____
Signature of Server

General Instructions

Anyone NOT A PARTY to the action, who is over the age of 18 may serve the Subpoena.

1. Find the person to be served (the witness)
2. Give the person a copy of the subpoena and the witness fees.
3. Serve a copy of the subpoena on every other party who has appeared
4. Fill out an Affidavit of Service for each person served, including the witness
5. Give all the affidavits of service to the person on whose behalf the subpoena was served for further proceedings in case the witness does not comply with this subpoena.

FREE CIVIL COURT FORM
No fee may be charged to fill in this form
CIV-GP-70 (Reverse) (Revised 7/09)

CIVIL COURT OF THE CITY OF NEW YORK

County of _____

_____ Part _____

Index No.: _____

_____
_____
                              Plaintiff(s)

-against-

_____
_____
                              Defendant(s)

STIPULATION TO ADJOURN

At the request of _____

and upon the consent of the parties hereto, the undersigned do hereby stipulate and agree that the:

☐ examination of the judgment debtor

☐ motion to punish the judgment debtor for contempt

☐ traverse hearing

☐ supplementary proceeding

☐ other _____

in the above-captioned action shall be adjourned to Special Term, Part _____, of the Civil Court

of the City of New York, County of _____ located at _____

_____ Room _____, on _____ at _____ a.m.,

or as soon thereafter as counsel may be heard.

_____
Signature of Plaintiff or
Attorney for Plaintiff

Telephone No.: (___) _____

_____
Signature of Defendant or
Attorney for Defendant

Telephone No.: (___) _____

_____
Signature of Other Party

_____
(Title of Status in Action)

Telephone No.: (___) _____

CIV-GP-92(Replaces Forms 4 & 5) (Revised 1/04)

Civil Court of the City of New York

COUNTY OF _____

_____
         Part

Index No. _____

_____

         Claimant(s), Plaintiff(s),

STIPULATION OF SETTLEMENT
and
AFFIDAVIT UPON DEFAULT

-aga ins t-

_____

         Defendant(s).

STIPULATION OF SETTLEMENT

It is hereby agreed by and between the parties that this claim is settled for the sum of $ _____ , to be

                                                                (Amount)

paid by _____ , on or before _____ to _____ at:

         (Debtor)   (Date)   (Creditor)

                                                                or as follows:

_____

                    (Address)

Upon such payment all parties shall be released from liability to each other concerning the matters in this dispute.

In the event Debtor fails to make payment as agreed to above, Creditor, upon completing the Affidavit below setting forth such default, shall be entitled to: *(SELECT ONE OPTION)*

☐   a) enter Judgment, without further notice to the Debtor, for the amount (originally sued for/agreed to above) less any payments made, together with interest and disbursements. (Cross out inapplicable choice)

☐   b) restore the case to the calendar for trial.

_____   _____   _____   _____
Signature   Date   Signature   Date

_____   _____   _____   _____
Signature   Date   Signature   Date

AFFIDAVIT UPON DEFAULT OF STIPULATION

State of New York, County of _____   SS:

_____ , being duly sworn, deposes and says:

                    (Creditor)

This case was settled as indicated above. The Debtor has failed to comply with the terms of the settlement. I,

_____

                    (Specify your request)

Sworn to before me this

_____ day of _____ 20_____

_____   _____
(Notary Public or Court Employee and Title)   Signature of Deponent

CIV-GP-31-*i* (Revised 1/03)

CIVIL COURT OF THE CITY OF NEW YORK
County of New York

Index Number ....

Request for Preliminary
Conference

Appearances:

....

Plaintiff(s)

Plaintiff ....

against

....

Defendant(s)

Defendant(s) ....

....

....

The Plaintiff requests a preliminary conference as required by rule 208.9.

Date Issue Joined: ....

Case Type (select one)
- [ ] No fault case
- [ ] Other (as authorized by the Administrative Judge) - List type ....

Please answer the following questions:

	Yes	No
Has a demand for the bill of particulars been served?	[ ]	[ ]
Has a bill of particulars been served?	[ ]	[ ]
Have medical reports and authorizations been furnished?	[ ]	[ ]
Has a physical examination been conducted?	[ ]	[ ]
Have all examinations before trial been completed?	[ ]	[ ]

What outstanding issues need to be resolved to allow this case to be put on the trial calendar?

....

....

....

....

By:

Date: ....

....

Attorney for Plaintiff

Part 27 Court Date (to be assigned by the Clerk) ....

CIV-GP-130-*i* (December 2005)

CIVIL COURT OF THE CITY OF NEW YORK
County of New York
Part 27 ....

Index Number ....

                    Plaintiff(s),

       -against-

               Defendant(s).
....

Preliminary Conference
Stipulation and Order
For Discovery

(Choose One)

☐ A. It is hereby stipulated and agreed that the entire action has been settled.
☐ B. It is hereby stipulated and agreed that all discovery has been complied with and no appearance is required in Part 27 on
☐ C. It is hereby (stipulated and agreed and) ordered at the preliminary conference that the following discovery issues will be complied with:

(Check all that apply)

☐ 1. Demand for bill of particulars to be served by: ....
☐ 2. Bill of particulars to be served by
☐ 3. Supplemental bill of particulars as to items ....
                                to be served by
☐ 4. Bill of particulars as to affirmative defenses to be served by
☐ 5. Authorizations for medical reports and/or records to be served by
☐ 6. Hospital authorizations to be served by
☐ 7. Physical examination of .... to be held on ....
    at
☐ 8. Copy of physician's report to be furnished to Plaintiff within .... days of examination.
☐ 9. Deposition of .... to be held on .... at
☐   Deposition of .... to be held on .... at
☐   Deposition of .... to be held on .... at
☐ 10. Other:
    ....
    ....
    ....

....
Date   Plaintiff's Attorney   Date   Defendant's Attorney

Compliance Conference scheduled for Part 28 on .... at .... am /pm.

Notice of Trial to be filed no later than ....

All dispositive motions shall be filed no later than .... days after filing the Notice of Trial.

So Ordered:

....
....
Date   Judge, Civil Court

CIV-GP-131-*i* (January, 2006)   FREE CIVIL COURT FORM
No fee may be charged to fill in this form.
Form can be found at: http://www.nycourts.gov/courts/nyc/civil/forms.shtml.

CIVIL COURT OF THE CITY OF NEW YORK
County of New York Part 28

Index Number ....

....

Plaintiff(s),

-against-

**Compliance
Stipulation and Order**

Defendant(s).

....

   ☐ A. It is hereby stipulated that the entire action has been settled.

   ☐ B. It is hereby (stipulated and agreed by the parties and) ordered that all outstanding
       discovery has been complied with.

No appearance will be required in Part 28 on ....

The Plaintiff /Defendant will file the Notice of Trial by ....

....	....	....	....
Date	Plaintiff s Attorney	Date	Defendant's Attorney

So Ordered:

....

      Date   Judge, Civil Court

CIV-GP-132-*i* (December, 2005)

About the Authors

Robert L. Lewis, Esq.

Robert L. Lewis, Esq. is an attorney who has specialized in the collection of bad debts in New York City for almost 30 years through his creditors' rights and commercial litigation practice. The Law Offices of Robert L. Lewis are located at 315 West 70th Street, New York, N.Y. 10023, and their main telephone number is: (646) 753-0450

Abraham J. Perlstein, Esq.

Abraham J. Perlstein is an attorney with broad legal practice which includes the collection of bad debts, commercial litigation, and commercial and technology contracts. The Law Office of Abraham J. Perlstein, Esq. is located at 1546 East 22nd Street Brooklyn, N.Y. 11210 and the main number is (212) 858-9289